Ethics VIOLENCE & Revolution

CHARLES C. WEST

Ethics

VIOLENCE

& Revolution

COMMENTARY BY
MONIKA HELLWIG
ERNEST W. LEFEVER

Published by the Council on Religion and International Affairs

Charles C. West went to China as a United Presbyterian Church missionary in 1947 and held posts in Germany and Switzerland before joining the Princeton Theological Seminary faculty as Professor of Christian Ethics. He is author of *Communism and the Theologians, Outside the Camp* and, with Robert C. Mackie, *The Sufficiency of God: Essays in Honor of Dr. W. A. Visser 't Hooft.*

Ernest W. Lefever is a member of The Brookings Institution Senior Foreign Policy Studies Staff. Among his varied publications are *Ethics and United States Foreign Policy, Arms and Arms Control* and, most recently, *Uncertain Mandate: Politics of the U.N. Congo Operation.*

Monika Hellwig is Assistant Professor of Theology at Georgetown University and a frequent contributor of articles and reviews to such periodicals as *Theological Studies, worldview, America, World Mission, Washington Service* and *Cross Currents.*

Contents

ETHICS, VIOLENCE AND REVOLUTION

Charles C. West

"The problem of Christian ethics," wrote Dietrich Bonhoeffer from the midst of his engagement in conspiratorial
resistance to the government of Adolf Hitler, "is the realization among God's creatures of the revelational reality of God
in Christ. . . . The place which in all other ethics is occupied
by the antithesis of 'should be' and 'is,' idea and accomplish-
ment, motive and performance, is occupied in Christian
ethics by the relation of reality and realization, past and
present, history and event, or, to replace the many meanings
of the concept with the name of the thing itself, the relation
of Jesus Christ and the Holy Spirit. . . . Good is reality itself,
reality seen and recognized in God."[1]

With this statement Bonhoeffer has made a confession of
his own relation to and response to reality. But he has also
defined a method by which ethics is done, a method which,
though rooted in Biblical history and the witness of the
Church, has also found in recent times humanistic expressions
which are influenced by that history and that witness. John
Dewey may find reality in human interaction and experiment,
Karl Marx may find it in the messianic proletariat, but in

[1] *Ethics* (New York, 1955), pp. 57, 59.

both cases — for liberals and radicals alike — the realization of that which has been revealed, and in relation to which we now stand, is the essence of ethics. It is the first and basic thesis of this essay that we cannot understand the phenomena of revolution and of violence, or come to terms with our responsibility toward them, except by this method. The variable which we have to examine is not our differing ideas of the ought or the good, but our understanding of and relation to the reality which governs our present and prepares our future. We live in a world where the greatest violence may be done by those who most condemn the word, and contrariwise, where the rhetoric of violence may cover the softest hearts and the most ineffectual actions. Revolutions are made often by the powers of the establishment while revolutionaries fight for the dismantling of new constructions in the name of freedoms and human values out of the past. These things happen between people who talk past each other while they struggle because they share no consensus about the context of their common world.

So it is especially with the American ethos as we face the decade of the 1970's. We confront the problem of violence and revolution in a passionate ambiguity which hides from us, not so much the abstract values about human life which we all affirm, but the real powers of this world with which we must deal, and the actual state of our relations with our neighbors. Our ethics are rooted in our ideologies. They reflect the divided state of our society, and our efforts to claim objectivity for them constitute attempts to justify ourselves over against those whose basic experience of reality differs from our own. The task of this essay then will not be to

8

elaborate principles and rules from the perspective of a relatively prosperous threatened Protestant white American for the condemnation, the prevention, the redirection, or even — as *ultima ratio* — the justification of violent revolution. It will rather be to penetrate as sensitively as possible the experience and ideology of those who are outside the structures in which the writer and many readers find security and hope, so that, in dialogue with them, we may discern the reality which offers a meaningful future to us both. The task has three parts: I. an examination of the peculiar context in which we as Americans understand and experience social reality, II. an exploration of the context of revolutionary experience and ideology, and III. some reflections which will start from the hypothesis that Bonhoeffer may be right about reality in his confession, and will probe what this might mean for the action of a Christian community which shares his faith.

I.

The ethos of American society, it is almost truistic to remark, differs from the standard conservative-radical tension in most of the world because the American tradition is not rooted in pre-modern culture claiming a sacred dimension and essential validity for its structure. From the beginning, an historical dynamic has been built into our society which is shared to a degree by other Anglo-Saxon countries but which distinguishes us sharply — to the point of mutual incomprehension — from many another nation, even from those we label Communist. The fact that the United States functions as the leading bulwark of conservatism in most of the world today is a fact which we lack the categories to understand, because the vocabulary of change, even including the word "revolution," is built into our self-image. The fact that there are people working for the transformation of American society and for world justice while maintaining loyalty to our basic political institutions is beyond the grasp of many a foreigner because he can see these institutions only through the ruling oligarchy of his own country, present or past.

This would not be so serious a misunderstanding, however, if our own society were not internally ambivalent at just the point with which this study is concerned. The name of this ambivalence is liberalism, in a broad, inclusive sense of the word: the belief that progress toward a future of indeterminate possibilities for mankind is an immanent tendency of human history; the belief that it is institutionalized in provisions which our political and economic structures make for individual freedom and initiative and for adjustment of old powers to new vitalities. It has, I suggest, two dimensions, both of them derivations, in a sense adaptations, of Christian themes to a humanist faith.

First, citizens of the United States see their society as a covenant. It was founded at a moment in history by people who had made an exodus. The direct experience of a deliberate break with the past in order to establish a new society, and a sense of the rightness of such a break has imparted itself to our tradition from its beginning. The real American revolution was the settling of America by groups who came here out of protest against conditions in the world from which they came, in hopes of realizing a promise given them by their faith: the Pilgrims and Puritans of New England, the Baptists of Rhode Island, the Quakers and Moravians of

10

Pennsylvania, and the Catholics of Maryland. The early New Englanders especially, as H. Richard Niebuhr has shown in *The Kingdom of God in America,* developed a clear theology of discontinuity — between the saving power of God and the structures of the political commonwealth — which was never allowed to relapse into dualism. The people who came to this country to found a church in which they might worship God faithfully and appropriately until the time of Christ's coming again, also sought to express their obedience in structures of the common life. But these structures were relative, limited, even experimental. They were endowed with no sacred validity of their own. They were constantly subject to the scrutiny which a Reformed consciousness of the danger of human power and pride required. At the same time they were instruments of hope which was not grounded in their own power or efficiency, but in a serious grasp of the promise of God for the whole life of man. In the words of the Declaration of Independence, these instruments might be "altered or abolished" when they obstructed that promise, to make way for new and different ones. Suspicion of unchecked power, readiness to change structures to tackle new problems, and hope that the future will vindicate the risk of faith this involves, are all the heritage of this initiative.

Americans are heirs to yet another lively tradition which is also covenantal, but continuous with the English background out of which our nation came, and party to all the ambiguities of that society. For John Locke, whose philosophy, expressed by Thomas Jefferson, turns up among other places in the Declaration of Independence, society is also a covenant, but the covenant takes the form of a contract among individuals to protect and further the "life, liberty and estate," which they have already as rights in the state of nature given by God. This state of nature has, in Locke's view, a law perceived by reason, "that all being equal and independent, no one ought to harm another in his life, health, liberty or possessions." Locke does not hesitate to place man by this law in the context of a will and purpose superior to his own: "for men, being all the workmanship of one omnipotent and infinitely wise Maker, all the servants of one sovereign Master, sent into the world by His order and about His business, they are his property, whose workmanship they are made to last during His, not one another's pleasure."[2]

This law and its divine Guarantor hold a somewhat paradoxical position in Locke's thought as a whole, however. He is an uncompromising empiricist, individualist, and nominalist in his theory of knowledge. There are in man no innate ideas. Thought starts from sensations, and universal concepts are abstractions designed to communicate the state of mind of one individual to another. They are a kind of mental contract, analogous to the social contract which leads to government. So also Locke is an egoistic hedonist in his view of human life. Rights are parallel to sensations, and are expressed in the power of the individual to master nature by labor for his personal fulfillment, which is property. Individual liberty and property is basic; it is assumed that the common good will arise out of the contract arrangements men make in the pursuit of their private interests and that this will correspond to a natural law intuitively known and rationally demonstrated. In the words of the Declaration of Independence:

2 *Of Civil Government,* Book II, Chapter II, 4 & 6.

"We hold these truths to be self-evident: that all men are created equal, that they are endowed by their Creator with certain unalienable rights, and that among these rights are life, liberty, and the pursuit of happiness. To secure these rights, governments are instituted among men."

This is all, of course, far from self-evident. It is in fact a momentous statement of faith, a confession of a certain ethical understanding of reality and of the relation of the believer to that reality, as it runs its historical course. In Locke's writing it reflects the peculiar ethos of the English settlement of 1688, but it has had several restatements since then. It is at the heart of Adam Smith's moderate theory of laissez-faire capitalism. It undergirded Jeffersonian democracy. It inspired John Stuart Mill and his American followers, and operated in the twentieth century in the pragmatism of Franklin D. Roosevelt. But its peculiarly American form has always been a combination of the two streams we have described: (1) empirical rational individualism along with a messianic consciousness of the destiny of a people so organized, (2) a belief in the saving power of the democratic process itself. It is this blend that has given American liberalism the resiliency to survive continual refutations of its basic premises by social experience and to define itself anew without losing the core of its optimism.

The covenant we understand ourselves to be formed by is expressed in our constitution and in a selective reading of the ethos which produced it. God functions not as a Biblical judge and redeemer of this relation but as the guarantor of the immanent process whereby a democratic people solve the problems of their common life and bring forth freedom, prosperity and peace for themselves and the world under constitutional guidance. Our understanding of the process is far less bland today than was John Locke's. A heavy dose of conflict theory has been injected into it, first by social Darwinism, then by Reinhold Niebuhr's understanding of the operation of human sin in the form of social power, and thirdly by the exigencies of the extra-legal struggle of organized labor for justice and acceptance. No modern defender would deny the danger that it may fall victim to absolutists of the left or right if democrats lose their courage and hope. All would recognize that the conditions of independent smallness which both Adam Smith and Thomas Jefferson regarded as essential to freedom and democracy have long since been left behind. But through it all the faith survives that there is an inherent genius in an "open society" — where powers balance each other, where public planning and private enterprise maintain a dynamic tension, where civil rights enforced by the courts protect minorities but the majority rules through the electoral process — which provides the only hope of avoiding destruction and bringing forth peace, justice, and a better life for man.

This faith, then, defines what is regarded in a liberal society as violent. Violence is harm done to another outside the rules of conflict which such a society sets up. It may even be the redress of grievances by means which the society does not permit. For example, the occupation of a building by sit-in protestors may be regarded as violence, but not the planned eviction of the tenants from their homes at the expiration of their leases so that the landlord can tear the building down for his profit. Again, if the government of a poor country

14

confiscates without compensation a foreign-owned business, its action may be called violent, while the owner's systematic retention of that disproportionate profit from his enterprise, which led to the action, will not be so labelled. It is not that the injustices of eviction or exploitation are unrecognized. But the creed of liberal society asserts that these injuries can be overcome by the channels of political action, legal suit and economic competition which the structure provides or can be brought to provide by moderate pressure. Revolution is not ruled out as an option when particularly intransigent and brutal tyrants obstruct the process. But it is the *ultima ratio* of social action whose purpose must be not to change the social system but, as Hannah Arendt has put it, to restore the constitutional freedom within which conflict would then be relativized and channels for self-development provided.[3]

Americans, on the whole, still believe in this covenant and regard as violent those forms of action which fall outside of it. But liberalism today has that *second* dimension which both reinforces and raises problems for this faith. We see our society not only as a process guided for good by some hidden Providence, but also as a construction of the human intelligence, developing in principle unlimited possibilities for human self-expression. Charles Beard a generation ago suggested that revolution is too mild a word to apply to this dynamic for "it implies that one order has been overturned and another substituted for it." But this is an episodic way of looking at change which really makes stability the norm. Rather we have "the beginning of an evolution of indefinite scope, bound by no reach of time. . . . In dealing with the

[3] *On Revolution* (New York, 1963), p. 140ff.

15

effects of technology upon social evolution we are not confronted by accomplished work alone, but also by a swiftly advancing method for subduing material things."[4] Or, in the words of Emmanuel Mesthene of Harvard, we have come to the point today where nature, which had always been man's limit, is now subject to his planning and inventing capacities.

We have the power and the will to probe and change physical nature, to control our own biology and that of the animals and plants in our environment, to modify our weather, to alter human personality, to reach the moon today and the rest of the heavens tomorrow. No longer are God, the human soul, or the mysteries of life improper objects of inquiry. . . . By creating new possibilities we give ourselves new choices. With more choices we have more opportunities. With more opportunities we can have more freedom, and with more freedom we can be more human. That, I think, is what is new about our age. We are recognizing that our technical prowess literally bursts with the promise of new freedom, enhanced human dignity, and unfettered aspiration.[5]

This development is the result of human planning. It is therefore an indefinite extension of the present centers of power which can finance, use, and control what science discovers and technology produces. It will "revolutionize" human living, but it will not be, in the political and social sense of the word as used in this essay, revolutionary. On the contrary

[4] Introduction to J. B. Bury, *The Idea of Progress* (Gloucester, Mass., 1960).

[5] "Religious Values in an Age of Technology," *Theology Today* (January, 1967).

16

it may, as André Philip suggests, have made political revolution obsolete and violence a futile, self-defeating gesture.[6] Only piecemeal change is possible in the direction of this process, by experts who have mastered some aspect of it and are humane enough to direct it toward broader and juster goals than would normally occur to the holders of power themselves.

One can indeed argue, as Zbigniew Brzezinski does, and as Mesthene evidently believes, that the same genius operates in the technocratic process as the liberals find in democratic politics — toward a meritocracy of the intellectual elite and toward greater participation by people at lower levels in decision making through increased communications, both processes eventually reaching down to include and raise up even the poorest in the nation and the world.[7] Certainly, as Harvey Cox, drawing on Barth, von Rad and others has shown, the control and management of nature by man is both a promise and a commandment from God, for nature was never intended to exist apart from and out of relation to the covenant promise which guides human history. The Christian, says the Apostle Paul, is by grace the steward of "the economy of the mystery hidden for ages in God who created all things" (Ephesians 3:9). But there is also another Biblical image which is more disturbing in the light it sheds on this development — the image of the tower of Babel. The problem with those first builders of an economic and technological order was not in their construction as such but in the purpose and motivation

[6] Ed. Z. K. Matthews, *Responsible Government in a Revolutionary Age* (New York and London, 1966), p. 120ff.

[7] *America in the Technetronic Age,* School of International Affairs, Columbia University, Occasional Paper, 1967, pp. 17-20.

of their building: "Come, let us build ourselves a city, and a tower with its top in the heavens, and let us make a name for ourselves, lest we be scattered abroad on the face of the whole earth" (Genesis 11:4). Then, as now, it was suggested that the process of technological development itself has a saving power, that it is itself the reality which has to determine our ideas of the good. And then, as now, we have had to learn the hard way that it is not so.

Like the Babelites, we are experiencing in liberal American society a confusing of our moral language and a scattering of our consensus. We speak of the boundless possibilities of a cybernated or technetronic economy, but the disparity in incomes within the United States, already the greatest in the industrialized world, increases every year, and the squalor of the cities grows greater. We speak of world development, but the production gap between the industrialized nations and those of the Third World grows annually. We speak of integration of races, and of growing interdependence in the community of mankind, but there is greater segregation of races in the United States now than ten years ago, and the industrial nations of the Western world find themselves increasingly disengaged from dependence on, and often from involvement in the world of Asia, Africa and Latin America. We speak of democratic social reform on behalf of the poor, but in this country the work of the anti-poverty program is a mere gesture toward a growing problem, and overseas our foreign aid program has dwindled, our support for foreign governments is more influenced by their reliability as our supporters than by the enlightenment of their domestic policies, and we are best known for the influence of private American business

18

interests and the intervention of our military. The result of all this is a growing distrust by outsiders not only of American power, but of the principles by which our country claims to operate and guide its policies, combined with our inner doubts and fears about their effectiveness. Violence seems to be no longer an external danger but a condition in which we live, in our cities at home, and in trying to keep or restore order in parts of the world as far away as Vietnam. The price of maintaining our liberal ethos seems to be the denial of its reality. In this context we can understand, perhaps, the ethos of the revolutionary.

II.

In simplest terms a revolutionary is one who has experienced this inner crisis of liberal society from the other side. He is not one whose security and hope are threatened by the violent implications of his own power for his ideals, but the object and victim of power which has destroyed his old securities in the name of a new promise which has never been realized. He is, to use Hegel's and Marx's term, alienated from that which defines him as a human being, alienated by the powers which are using him for their ends. He has no stake in the social order under which he lives. He is its living negation, and in this negation he finds his hope and the motive for his action. Reality is in his experience a process of structured institutionalized violence which is moving toward a destruction beyond which is a new and more humane order.

This description has at least three distinguishable parts, all of which owe their classic definition to Marx, but are also rooted in Biblical and Christian origins. *First,* revolution is a dynamic condition in man's relation to social existence, to

19

the means of production and their organized distribution. It is not the condition of poverty in and of itself. It is not even the process of impoverishment as such. Here many refutations of the subordinate Marxist thesis of the growing impoverishment of the proletariat miss the point. Revolutionary conditions are created by a combination of the breakdown of old structures of communal security with the creation of vast new possibilities for human life which the dispossessed can see, but which they cannot realize because the dynamics of power work against them.[8]

[8] Admittedly this is a post-Marxist definition. Crane Brinton, for one, maintains in *Anatomy of Revolution* (rev. ed.; New York, 1957) that revolution is perpetrated by classes which are rising in prosperity, are dynamic in their economic and social potential, against the irrationality and arbitrary injustice of old structures. This pattern is taken basically from the French Revolution. Hannah Arendt maintains in *On Revolution* that this revolution went wrong when, instead of following the American intention to set up a free constitutional system within which the social problem could be solved in a relative and pragmatic way, the French leaders found themselves caught up in the social question itself, with the result that the laws of historical necessity became the chief preoccupation of revolutionaries. But both of these analysts are trying to reduce the experience of revolution once again to liberal terms, the one by belittling the force of alienating and dehumanizing power, the other by finding in the "social question," where this power operates, only a demonic temptation to remake man at cost of his freedom. The basic criterion of revolution as we use it here is *discontinuity* between the revolutionary and the centers of power, and lack of channels in existing structures of politics, production or ideology for effecting change. The American Revolution was, by this criterion, what happened in the seventeenth not the eighteenth century. The "industrial" or "cybernetic" revolution, or the "revolution in weapons technology," are all misuses of the term because they all are projections and adjustments of present centers of power rather than their reversal.

This, however, is a mild way of putting what happens. When the power of modern imperialism — I use the term here to define the whole complex of powers having an ecumenical or universalizing impact, rather than a particular political-military-ideological movement — breaks into a hitherto stable self-contained society, the result is the attempted condensation into one or two generations of a development which in Western industrial society has been spread over 400 to 1000 years and at the same time the cramping and misdirection of this change. It would far exceed the scope of this paper to describe such conditions, but let two snapshots present the problem.

In China the power of foreign enterprise created a transportation system, centralized credit and land ownership, set up centers of industry which came to dominate the consumer market and thereby drew masses of population to the cities out of their traditional communities. It demonstrated real political power as distinct from the ancient system of suzerainty, tribute and ceremony by which China had been ruled. It opened up a vision of vast new human wealth and the hope of tremendous development. At the same time traditional patterns of social relations — family controls, village customs, with the social security they provided, the rewards and punishments which gave stability to a local subsistence economy almost without any system of formalized law — suddenly became irrelevant. They not only failed to provide the means of bringing order and meaning into the new world; they were increasingly unable to provide even the minimum of security for which they existed. The village became dependent on the city market. The local moneylender became

21

dependent on the central bank. Wars and rebellions which would not be mitigated by local bargaining swept over the countryside. Local reforms would not work because of the corruption which centralized control and increasing poverty breeds. Efforts by Chinese leadership to master and give direction to this vitality broke down time after time because the traditional values and structures of authority themselves undermined the development of new indigenous power. Concepts of family loyalty corrupted effective government at every level and undermined good business practice. Respect for age, status and scholarship made reforms in the interests of effective functioning and technological development often impossible. By 1947 public order itself had disintegrated, except in Communist controlled areas, to the extent that the basic protections of law were available only to those who could pay for them, or whose influence was such as to protect them.

In Brazil,[9] rapid economic development — the expansion of capital and the intensification of industry for example — has not been accompanied by the shifts in political power which would place decisions in the hands of broader sections of the people. International capitalism, rather than an indigenous middle class, to say nothing of local trade unionism, has set the tone. The result has been the enthronement of a bureaucratic class in economic and political control. The state has become the main economic agent supporting the

[9] I take this analysis primarily from the Brazilian economist Candido Mendes de Almeida, in his speech to the World Conference on Church and Society, Geneva, 1966. It is an analysis from one point of view and thus reflects the interaction between actual conditions of revolution and consciousness of these conditions — or ideology — with which we deal in the next point.

interests of this class, not those of national development as a whole. In most cases the common people remain permanently outside the industrial economy, or on the edge. of it, working at bare subsistence wages. The impoverished countryside provides a nearly endless supply of workers on these terms.

Thus the society stagnates and decays while it talks the language of evolutionary technological and economic development with its democratic political accoutrements. The market economy is maintained in theory but does not operate in practice because subsidies and state controls socialize the losses. The myth of traditional society emerging into the modern world covers the brute fact that the society is determined economically by world markets and local oligarchs, thus undermining any controlling and valuing influence tradition might have. The forms of democratic elections fail to offer real alternatives. The labor movement, the intelligentsia and the Church are all subverted by a combination of economic control and lack of hope. Control remains in the hands of an oligarchy which combines political, industrial-commercial, and a few intellectual leaders interested in the perpetuation of their power. It is, in the words of Candido Mendes, a mutually compensating system of atrophy, from which the only hope of escape lies in the development of a popular and revolutionary culture.

These are only two of the most flagrant examples. Similar descriptions could be provided of the condition of the black Africans in South Africa, Angola or Mozambique, the peasantry of the Philippines, or of the "culture of poverty" with its strong racial coloring in the United States. The point of them is not such descriptive objective accuracy as they may claim, but their reflection of an actual relation in which millions of people stand to the forces at work on their society, a relation with its roots in political and economic power and conditions, and its expression in analyses such as these.

This leads to the *second* distinguishing mark of revolution: it is a consciousness that conditions of exploitation, of dispossession and powerlessness need not and should not prevail, and that to be human is to separate oneself from them and struggle against them. "In the conditions of the proletariat," wrote Marx and Engels in *The Communist Manifesto,* "those of the old society are virtually swamped. The proletarian is without property; his relation to his wife and children has no longer anything in common with the bourgeois family relations; modern industrial labor, modern subjection to capital . . . has stripped him of every trace of national character. Law, morality, religion are to him so many bourgeois prejudices behind which lurk in ambush just as many bourgeois interests." The revolutionary is a man conscious of a basic alienation of his true being from the conditions of the society under which he lives. He is its active, living negation.

Revolution is, then, a state of consciousness which defines the existing structure of law and order — the existing balance of power — as violence, and is devoted to its basic overthrow. It is, in other words, an ideology. It can therefore be dismissed as misanthropy or denounced as the destructive will of disordered people. But it is also the fundamental question to every structure of self-justification which those who profit by existing structures of power and order throw up to defend themselves against the claims of the weak and the outcast.

It is therefore the nemesis of ideology, the penultimate question mark set against social and political achievement which gives promise to some and not to others. It is the reminder to every system which claims to incorporate provisions for new vitalities — for shifts in power and changes in direction — into its own dynamic, that its very pretension to this openness may well be a clever means of maintaining present structures and preventing any basic change at all. It is the proletarian's testimony to the fact of his basic alienation and to the violence being done him by the powers that be.

This proletarian is therefore both a material and a spiritual stranger to the society in which he lives. Physical conditions may prepare him, but, as Arnold Toynbee has shown in his analysis of the breakdown of civilizations, it is the spiritual break which makes him a fundamental subversive. Indeed his alienation may result not from his own physical suffering but from disillusion with the injustice of a system from which even he profits and a conviction that it is morally condemned. From the moment he says "no" (if we follow Camus in *The Rebel*) to the whole sacred system of ideas and physical relations which previously explained and ordered his very being in subjection to it — whether he was a perpetrator or a victim of violence in that system — he becomes a human being, and starts to participate in the true community of mankind.

From this follows however the *third* mark of the revolutionary without which the negation makes no sense. He is a man of hope. He is in fact the complete penultimate eschatologist. He lives for the future. Every action and every institution, including those that maintain the tradition of revolutionary consciousness, is seen in terms of the goal toward which it is striving, not in terms of what it preserves and maintains. Because the revolutionary hopes so much, he hesitates to define the form of the goal toward which he is working. Liberation from existing structures is the first object. Then he will be a different kind of man, free to determine his course in new conditions. There are of course symbolic statements of the relations of the new society. "From each according to his ability, to each according to his need" was, according to Marx, to be inscribed on its banners. "The definitive resolution of the antagonism between man and nature, and between man and man — the true solution of the conflict between essence and existence, between objectification and self-affirmation, between freedom and necessity, between individual and species . . ."[10] is his more comprehensive picture. But all of this means only to say that in the new world, after the abolition of the present structures of power and the reversal of their present dynamic, the basic conflict of this society will no longer exist, and quite new relations will therefore be possible, which will be human, not inhuman. Then violence as a social condition will disappear.

We have said that revolution is a penultimate question mark and a penultimate eschatology. Like liberalism it too has Christian roots, and has turned a dimension of the covenant history into a self-validating explanation of the immanent meaning of history. The German Marxist philosopher Ernst Bloch is right in tracing its original impulse to the exodus of the Hebrew people from Egypt. There is found the pristine form of the "no" of an oppressed people who refused all

[10] Economic-Philosophical Manuscripts, in Erich Fromm, *Marxist Concept of Man* (New York, 1961), p. 127.

accommodation, all temptation to ideological-religious adjustment and reformist tactics, in the hope of a new society and by confidence in a new power which they could not define beforehand because they were to realize and discover them in the course of the revolt itself. This theme of exodus in hope has accompanied Hebrew-Christian history to this day, not only or even primarily as a geographical movement, but rather as a response to prevailing inhuman conditions in the light of their destruction and the coming of a new world. In the New Testament it was expressed in the resurrection of a Messiah who had been executed by the powers that be, his victory over these powers and the coming of his kingdom. Throughout the history of what Arend Theodoor van Leeuwen calls "the revolutionary West"[11] it has taken the form of an abrasive reminder to the powers and forms of an errant Christendom that they are not only subject to divine judgment for the injustices they incorporate but that their pretensions to sanctity compound their sin. It is also a stimulating reminder to the poor and the alienated that the promise of God is precisely for them and that they can be the bearers of the new and transformed reality which arises out of the death of the old. It is no accident that this history is not one of continuity but of continuing tension and conflict in which no one principle of order and no one worldview or social class could rule unchecked, and in which forces continually arose from below to challenge the reigning structure.

But there is also another sense in which the revolutionary tradition, which found its classic spokesman late in history in Karl Marx, is the ally and sometimes the rescuer of the Chris-

[11] *Christianity in World History* (New York, 1966), Ch. VI.

tian tradition. The theme of exodus in hope is constantly beset by two distortions. It has been diverted into the channels of nationalism and used to express the special grievance and the special hope of one tribe or race against the world: among the ancient Hebrews, but also among eighteenth- and nine-teenth-century Americans, among Afrikaners in South Africa, and among a few extremist Black nationalists today. And it has been far more often turned into metaphysical dualism, that classic religious device for grounding the lightning of social protest. Conservative and radical Christian movements alike have been guilty of this distortion. The consolations of an eternal realm of fulfilled dreams to compensate for the irreformable inhumanity of this world were not only offered by an established church, they undermined the prophetic pro-test of revolutionary forces as well. The monastic protest against Byzantine Christianity did not intend reform, al-though it had to build a new society after the Byzantine decline in Western Europe. The Communist Taborites of Bohemia and the radical reformers led by Thomas Müntzer sharply distinguished the saved from the lost and were not concerned for the latter. And even our seventeenth-century Puritan, Baptist and Quaker forebears, revolutionary as their actions and faith were, shared the sentiments which H. Richard Niebuhr quotes from Roger Williams: "O let us the reformed, beg grace from Heaven, that we may use earthly comforts as a stool or ladder to help us upward to heavenly comforts, profits, pleasures, which are only true and lasting, even eternal in God himself, when these Heavens and earth are gone."[12]

12 *The Kingdom of God in America* (New Haven, 1956), p. 50.

Over against all of this, revolutionary Marxism has reminded both theology and politics that the promise of God to the proletariat of this misdirected world is both temporal and universal. It has to do with the future, not with eternity, and it is concerned with a new humanity for all mankind. It is a promise which rejected and dispossessed humanity has the special qualifications to accept and fulfill, because the death being forced upon it prepares it to welcome the resurrection to come, which might appear to those who still have old securities to protect, as death.

It is at this point, however, that the internal dilemma of the revolutionary condition arises. When, in the course of human events, does the moment of revolution arrive? Which, since we are dealing with an immanent historical analysis and hope, is the moment of the eschaton when reality is transformed? When does the system of violence give way to the structure of human freedom and when are the powers of the establishment basically overthrown? There are at least four types of answers to this complex of questions given in revolutionary circles today. Let us look at them briefly in turn.

1. The conventional reply, on which most of us who have studied communism were raised, which bears the name of Stalin but is more properly Leninism, focuses on the moment when the Communist Party on behalf of the proletariat captures the machinery of state power. This is the resurrection. Before this moment the strategy and tactic of the Party is concerned with the conquest of this power according to the laws of history which it both incarnates and knows. It is a strategy of developing the inner contradictions of an imperialist-capitalist society toward its own destruction and of fur-

thering this destruction where possible. After this moment it is a policy of planned development to remake human society and therefore human nature in socialist countries while promoting the revolution abroad until the happy time arrives when institutions of compulsion are no longer necessary. Ethics and tactics are then identical, and the arbiter of both is the science of revolutionary development which the Party expresses. "Morality is that which serves to destroy the old exploiting society and to unite all the toilers around the proletariat which is creating a new, Communist society."[13]

It hardly need be added that this answer is discredited today, the more so the more it is used by *Pravda* to justify the invasion of Czechoslovakia and the repression of intellectual freedom in the Soviet Union long after the repudiation of Stalin. Ironically, Soviet ethics are repudiated in revolutionary circles today both because they justify inhuman violence and because they are complacently establishmentarian. The section on ideology, education and culture in the program of the XXII Congress of the Communist Party of the Soviet Union differs only in a few references to a "spirit of collectivism" from the ideals of a secular American liberal of the pragmatist school. But this only makes the question we have raised more acute.

2.   A substantial group of Marxists — perhaps a majority in the French and Italian Communist Parties, and certainly a majority in Czechoslovakia — have reinterpreted the whole function of class struggle, the meaning of alienation, and the process of human liberation. Alienation, the Polish philosopher Adam Schaff says flatly, is a continuing fact of society

[13] Lenin, "The Tasks of the Youth Leagues," 1921.

even under socialist organization because it is inherent in the necessities of the productive process itself. It may be relatively eliminated, by a continual process of improving the channels of participatory democracy in plants and offices, but ultimate freedom in the labor process is a limiting concept. Marxism, writes Roger Garaudy in France, is "a methodology of historical initiative" which allows the building of plural models of socialism. Revolutionary activity is a kind of aesthetic creativity wherein man struggles to realize himself against all the dehumanizing obstacles of capitalist exploitation but with those of other convictions, including Christians, who are concerned with human freedom. Milan Machovec, recently of Prague, goes a step further. A movement of dialogue — with the higher self and with the other who differs from the self — is essential to revolutionary activity, because in that activity I myself am transformed and discover what humanity truly is by risking myself in the encounter.

All of these men have answered our question by turning revolution into an ongoing, even a dialogic, process, not so different from an evolution. Their experience of self-righteous revolutionary power dehumanizing man is more immediate than that of capitalist oppression. On the firm basis of a socialist organization of production — which they all regard as a moral achievement in the elimination of arbitrary violence — they are prepared to come to grips with new misuses of power and above all with the relativity of their own concepts of what it means to be human.

3. For this very reason, however, a gulf opens up between these participants in the Marxist-Christian dialogue in Europe and revolutionaries, Marxist and Christian, in Africa and

Asia. The answer of these men turns in the opposite direction, toward a search for the pure revolutionary — the one who will truly resist all temptation to compromise his warfare against the all-pervading power of imperialist order. Frantz Fanon searches for him in vain among the peasants while he chronicles the betrayal of the revolution by one indigenous class after another. Castro and Guevara find him in the disciplined guerrilla, the member of a small cadre in the mountains who organizes and expands his operation until he gradually reaches the stage where he needs an ideology in order to take over the country. Both agree that the new man is born in violence; the violent act itself is therapeutic; only by this degree of self-assertion against the exploiter does the proletarian become aware of who he is and what he may become. What he will do with his power when he has thus established his humanity is a later question. First he must rebel, and in this rebellion a new community must arise.

But Fanon's book *The Wretched of the Earth* ends with a series of case studies in the psychological disorder created by the violence and counter-violence of the Algerian war, and no real hope. Probably he, the Cuban ideologists, and some of the Chinese represent the purest examples of proletarian consciousness as Marx imagined it a century ago. It is reflected also in some expressions of the Black Panthers and the Students for a Democratic Society in this country. But we are seeing movements steeped in this consciousness destroy themselves while they leave our question unanswered.

4. There is a fourth group to which one could give the loose label of anarchism. These are people who have seen through the illusion of revolutionary power as a whole. They

trust it no more than any other kind. Centralized authority and power are themselves the enemy and they like them as little in their own organization as anywhere else. Rudi Dutschke in Berlin develops this point of view into a philosophy of society not very different from the nineteenth-century anarchism of Proudhon, based on decentralized communities where the economic and social functions of life are carried on with a minimum of compulsion and a maximum of participation in the decision-making processes. Carl Oglesby's working principle states it with defiant eloquence:

> The socialist radical, the corporatist conservative and the welfare-state liberal are all equally capable of leading us forward into the totalized society. Whether central planning should be coordinated by government or corporate hands is a question whose realism has disappeared. The urgent question is about the locus of power in the community: Is it in the state or is it in the people? The main principle of the radically humanist politics is this: *Any decision not made by the people in free association, whatever the content of that decision, cannot be good.* If the American humanist must mellow his intransigence and move from his utopian principles to meet the realities of life in the technological society, it is nevertheless that main principle which sets his goals, gives him style, and motivates his work.[14]

Violence may still play a role in the action of those who share this conviction, but it is the violence of the demonstra-

[14] In *Containment and Change: Two Dissenting Views of American Society and Foreign Policy* by Oglesby and Richard Shaull (New York, 1967), p. 164; Oglesby's italics.

tion, not of the guerrilla movement. It is the application of extra-legal, not necessarily illegal force, to bring about the decentralization of the decision-making process in one segment of society — as with the Berlin student riots last year — or to demonstrate by provocation the covert violence already present in the forces of law and order — as in Chicago in the summer of 1968. The basic trend of this answer to the question of revolution however is away from large-scale action toward the formation of new communities in whose style of life the promise of a new society may be born. These communities are not regarded as "dropping out." They are a part of the social dynamic, and are subversive of existing power structures in quite concrete ways: by supporting resistance to the selective service system and the Vietnam war, by dramatizing and helping the fight of the poor and the blacks *as communities* to determine their own future, and above all by demonstrating in their own common life a freedom from economic temptations and pressures — a practice of mutual support — which will suggest the form of the new human relations they seek. They express the revolutionary experience, in short, in a utopian form, as the word "utopian" is interpreted by Martin Buber: the promise of the new society already taking form in the old which it will one day replace, subordinating in the process the questions of power to the question of humanizing function.

That this, too, is no answer to the problem of revolutionary change will be obvious to every reader who has studied the history of utopian communities in the light of human nature. But it does at least pose a fundamental question for Christian ethics. Given the insight, which we have now traced in both its liberal and its revolutionary forms, that human community is threatened by the very power used to defend or realize it because its very principles of universal validity perpetrate violent exclusion upon some, is there a reality which includes and corrects us all, and if so what might its content be?

III.

We return to the premise of this essay, which both of the perspectives we have described share with the Christian and Jewish faiths: reality is not an ultimate structure, but a covenantal relation. Ethics are then reflections on human response to that relation in the light of the promise it bears, the power it reveals and the humanity it defines and brings forth. Action, also on the political level, is basically witness to this reality, this power and this promise which we trust to prevail, even though, in our anxiety, we may sometimes act as if we ourselves were its defenders and guarantors. If then we presume, as Christians must, that this reality is the God who made himself known in the covenant history whose heart is the life, death and resurrection of Jesus Christ, what are its consequences for our political action and understanding? I suggest three basic propositions.

*   *   *

1. *First,* the primary movement of the covenant of God with man is not, Ernst Bloch the Marxist and many a Lutheran to the contrary, rebellion disciplined by law, but promise, grace and freedom in the context of which man discovers and explores what it means to be and prosper as a human being in community with his neighbors. The first of the ten commandments, which governs all the others, is not a pro-

hibition but the statement of a gift: "I am the Lord thy God who brought thee up out of the land of Egypt, out of the house of bondage; thou shalt have no other gods before me." Man is to accept this relation, to grow in it, love it and pass its grace on to others. He is to enjoy and create human community which expresses this covenant relation on earth with its historical direction and purpose, to be a blessing for "all the families of the earth." The direction of it is outward — toward the poor and the excluded — as well as forward toward fuller development of the human and natural resources of the earth. The form and quality of it are defined by Christ.

The dynamic of this relation then defines in the first instance what constitutes violence and its opposite, the act of loving. Violence is what bars the way to this reality for another, excludes him from it and breaks the human relation through which he might come to understand and accept it. It is more often expressed in neglect of the neighbor than in an overt act. In American society its most common expressions are in the conditions produced by the "natural" results of private interests pursuing their ends; pressure groups lobbying for their interests, and exclusive communities seeking to maintain an ethos of congeniality and peace. "The natural," says Bonhoeffer, "is that which, after the Fall, is directed toward the coming of Christ. The unnatural is that which, after the Fall, closes its doors against the coming of Christ."[15] In other words existence, nature, peace, are not given structures upon which man then operates. They reflect human action from the beginning — man's violence or his planned creative love.

15 Bonhoeffer, *op. cit.*, p. 102.

It follows that response to covenant reality requires of a Christian that he take responsibility for organizing his world so as to realize its promise. This requires among other things political action governed by a concept of the form this promise might take. With this, the basic question of the relation of political power — the compulsory function of the state — to the realization of true human community is raised. There can be no doubt that at this stage in history the political authority is neither God nor the Church. Christian history, since the encounter of Jesus with Pilate, has been concerned both to legitimate and to limit the political function clearly. Nevertheless I believe that those theologians are mistaken who have, with Luther, defined the state as "God's hangman" and confined it to the negative task of restraining the grosser consequences of human sin by a merciless law. Government has, on the contrary, an external, relative, but very real relation to the whole positive purpose of human community which is given its form in Christ — in other words, to the redemption of man.

"First of all then," writes Paul to Timothy, "I urge that supplications, prayers, intercessions, and thanksgivings be made for all men, for kings and all who are in high positions, that we may lead a quiet and peaceable life, godly and respectful in every way. This is good, and it is acceptable in the sight of God our savior who desires all men to be saved and to come to the knowledge of the truth" (I Timothy 2:1-4). Politics is therefore a creative, even a redemptive task. It is aimed at creating a relative justice and order in a chaotic world so that men may be liberated to respond to the higher tasks of human community to which they are called.

It is ordained to counteract and curb the violence defined above by participating, with its compulsory function, in the responsible planning and ordering of nature and human relations toward the inclusion of all the outcast in the promise of justice and love which the covenant offers. The state cannot *do* this job, because its function is general and compulsory not personal and voluntary, but it can help create the conditions which enable it to be done. This has, I believe, three consequences for our theme:

A. The state will operate in this task, inevitably, with a positive concept of what constitutes and leads to human justice and freedom. This concept will be ideological. It will reflect the interests and perspectives of some groups and not others. This ideological bias is of course a serious matter since, unlike the Church, the Black Panthers, the Ku Klux Klan or Standard Oil, its decisions can be enforced in law. But a positive, explicit philosophy of what it means to love one's neighbor and how this should be embodied in particular policies is far more honest and creative than the pretension to neutrality, or a weakness which makes the state the football of conflicting lobbies. Only by embodying a particular conception of the public welfare can the government challenge opposing groups to state their case in terms of the public welfare rather than their private interests, thus relativizing and perhaps correcting the government's own understanding and policy. Only in such a debate do the groups in society which do not have power but whose rights and hopes are at stake, occupy the center of attention. Only then does the general interest — the interest of consumers, users of public facilities, breathers of the public air — come adequately into focus. Let me illustrate with two examples, one positive and one negative.

a. When, in 1947, Secretary of State Marshall launched the European Recovery Program, he did so with a sound and careful analysis of the long-term interest of both Europe and the United States, reaching out toward the welfare of the whole world. Conservative opposition was forced onto a larger stage than group or private interest, and left-wing opposition soon found itself isolated in its own ideological prison.

b. The Office of Economic Opportunity, with its philosophy of participation by the poor in planning for their own future, should have been a parallel case. But in fact the government did not press the philosophy against its opponents, and did not fund the Office adequately to do its job. Despite some success O.E.O. has been dismembered by interests on the right and disillusioned revolt on the left without a public debate or a new policy.

In short, America's revolutionaries, and this country's Third World revolutionary opponents, are as violent as they are in word or deed not so much because of the positively formulated philosophy of our government as because of the hidden interests and powers whom they see influencing real decisions which do violence to them, and who do not enter the arena of honest ideological debate. The revolutionaries sense rightly, that behind this refusal to articulate and be responsible for a clear policy lies a covert idolatry. Most of them misunderstand this idolatry as a single Moloch — the self-reinforcing establishment — whereas it is in fact a loose form of polytheism where various human interests are absolutized and coexist more or less tolerably with each other. But it is idolatry still, the characteristic sign of which is that it shies away from real theological-political exposure.[16]

B. When this has been said, the second and negative point must also be made which is, however, positive in another way. When the state asks seriously how to embody a positive concern for the development of human freedom into its laws, it is called to institutionalize opposition against itself as ideological agent. The most commonly used Old Testament concept of law is *torah,* whose basic meaning is teaching, instruction, or direction. It presupposes not a minimum standard which can be satisfied, leaving the rest of life to individual pleasures, but a continuing relationship the meaning of which is explored and expressed in dialogue. The question to which the *torah* is a continually experimental and ever-repentant answer is: how may God and the neighbor be effectively loved? In one dimension of its activity the state participates with its power to enable and compel, as we have seen, in the formulation of this answer. It is called to direct the economic and social energies of its people toward justice and freedom for all.

16 This would seem on the surface to be arguing on the side of John Foster Dulles against George Kennan in the famous debate about moral principles versus national interest in foreign policy. In fact, however, both men are on the author's side of this question. Kennan's warning was not against a coherent concept of the way in which national interest relates to the ecumenical interest of world peace and development, but against absolutizing that concept and therefore the cutting off of dialogue and adjustment with those whose interests and concepts differ. It was a reminder that the state is not God. Dulles' error was not in having a moral ideology but in not recognizing it as an ideology, which led him to question the moral integrity of those whose concepts differed from his own.

40

Despite the ideological bias of any particular government "the state alone has the power and the authority under God to act as trustee for society as a whole."[17]

In another dimension, however, precisely as trustee for society as a whole, the state has the function of restraining human power — including its own power — where that power would result in violence to others. It has the task of enabling and protecting the dialogue among groups in society about what justice and freedom are, which may well result in pressures to change government policy. About this function several things need to be said:

a. Although we are talking about the structure of a democratic state in an open society, this process can never be embodied once and for all in a given set of institutions. One can marvel at the capacity of the Supreme Court to adapt our constitutional tradition to the requirements of modern democracy. One can be grateful for the growing electoral power and shrewdness of black voters. But the clumsiness and expense of our legal system still leave the poor largely at its mercy and our Bill of Rights still does not protect the selective objector to the war in Vietnam. The political process still does not provide the channels for large but ill-organized minorities to make their grievances felt. There is a large and growing substratum of violence in our society, in which government among other powers participates, and which we have not yet learned how to order.

b. The object of the restraint of violence by the enforcement of law is the liberation of human beings for responsible

[17] II Assembly World Council of Churches, Evanston, 1954, Report of Section III.

41

relations with each other, not the maintenance of a rule as such, or the protection of property as such. From the earliest laws of the Old Testament down to the Puritans of seventeenth-century Massachusetts, no principle has been clearer than this. Yet at no point is there more blindness, hypocrisy and prejudice in modern society than here. The right to private property is an extension of the right of a man to self-protection and self-expression. This includes the right to decent housing, enough money to live on, and freedom from economic coercion and exploitation — rights the denial of which form the core of violence in our society today. To quote a man of experience in the subject, Mayor John Lindsay of New York before the 1968 Republican Convention's Resolutions Committee:

The poor are victims of an even more pervasive form of lawlessness [than crimes of violence in the streets]. Each day their lives are ordeals of quiet criminality. They are sold defective goods and inferior food at exorbitant prices; they are denied work because of the color of their skin; they are confined in houses that can murder a human being as surely, if not as swiftly, as a loaded gun. We should not be surprised if the poor are unimpressed by calls for law and order, for the law is what garnishes their wages, and an order is what evicts them from their homes.

When in response to this, or in outrage because of this kind of violence, demonstrations break out into riots and stores are looted, the first responsibility of government — the police first, then other officials — is to re-establish order and peace, to lower the level of violence, not to intensify it in the name of the law. The violence of a riot must be countered, however violent the conditions that produced it. But the agents of government, however provoked, ought never to exacerbate a violent situation with their own participation. This, if the Kerner Report is correct, is what happened in the Newark riots of 1967 and, I believe, in Chicago during the summer of 1968.

Secondly, violence against property is incommensurable with violence against persons. Former Attorney General Ramsey Clark touched on a basic principle when he maintained that looters should be arrested but on no account shot. Indeed, the degree of crime involved in attacks on property should be measured in terms of the injury done to persons, not in its own right.

c. In this context there can also be, before God, a responsible resistance to the unjust and violent application of law and governmental authority, to which the same considerations apply as to government itself. The issue is not violence or non-violence in this resistance, for the violence already exists — in a law which compels men against their conscience, for instance, to kill in Vietnam, or an eviction notice which is part of a plan to dispossess a community to build higher income housing. It is rather a question of intention and proportionality. If the function of government is as we have described it, the intention of resistance to the violence it perpetrates must be to purge and restore it to that function. It is resistance *against* the state as partisan power and *for* the state as ordering and liberating function. It is a means of recalling the state to that function. Therefore the means must also be appropriate to this end, and not to the further incitement of violence, even when these means themselves are violent. It is a dangerous half-truth which describes the urban riots of the black community as the chief source of the benefits which have since come to them. The truth is that without the organization of power, without the threat, if not the reality, of violent explosion, the consciences of white America would not have been sufficiently pricked and its fears sufficiently aroused to do anything. The falsehood is to ignore the fact that if this violence is further directed toward ends which destroy the fabric of the common life of which government is the guarantor altogether, white society will institutionalize its forms of violence against the blacks and all humanity will suffer.

C. Finally, the political function is, in the intention of God, ecumenical. The purpose and direction of the covenant community is outward toward all the excluded throughout the earth. Therefore no partial government — national, state, or local — has an absolute right to exist and perpetuate and defend itself. At the same time every government has, in proportion to its influence and power, a responsibility for exploring and realizing the same external conditions for human community between the nations that it seeks in the society under its own sovereignty.

"God's reconciliation in Jesus Christ," reads the United Presbyterian *Confession of 1967,* "is the ground of the peace, justice and freedom among nations which all powers of government are called to serve and defend. The church in its own life is called to practice the forgiveness of enemies and to commend to the nations as practical politics the search for cooperation and peace. This requires the pursuit of fresh and responsible relations across every line of conflict, even at risk to national security, to reduce areas of strife and to broaden international understanding."

This may seem like an impossible prescription for any existing government. There is no way by which foreigners can vote in American elections, and there is no magic by which American people can be brought to feel the interests of other peoples with the same intensity as their own. There is no reflection of the covenant in an enforceable system of international law, and therefore no earthly power to relativize the conflict of interests and ideologies, with due respect to the real but secondary accomplishments of the United Nations under the leadership of Dag Hammarskjöld.

But what we are here describing is not an impossible ideal. It is reality in the light of which interests are understood and hope formulated. At work behind the international conflict and compromise of forces itself is an intention which bears a promise for the nation, risks the relations and actions it requires and threatens destruction if ignored. What this implies is the substance of the next two points.

*   *   *

2. We come to our *second* basic proposition. The powers of this world organize around their own centers to defy and distort the purpose of God. But the result, Reinhold Niebuhr to the contrary, is not a perpetual dialectic of relative moral achievements, tentative orders and their breakdowns, in which the love and sacrifice of Christ remains an everlasting judgment and inspiration, but rather the continual demythologizing and disarming of the powers by God — more spe-

cifically by Christ — in order that they may be legitimized as servants of His purpose for man. This is why the power struggle is a legitimate area for the exercise of Christian responsibility. It is also why the Christian community continues in a fruitful tension with both political authorities and revolutionaries, though it may at times be denounced by the one as compromising and weak, and by the other as subversive and revolutionary. The task of the Christian is to be a witness within the political struggle to both the disarming and the legitimating process which operates within yet overrules the power conflict.

This means first a realistic and yet subtle and sensitive analysis of the actual powers at work in society. They are not simple expressions of one undifferentiated force. Their roots are in what Niebuhr calls the "vitalities" of life, the various creative urges to self-expression in all their qualitative variety and differing subjects. The Greek New Testament word *exousiai* catches this variety better than the English. The *exousiai* are proper forces in the world springing out of human desires, drives and hopes. But they have been hypostatized over against man and man has become enslaved to them. They are expressions of his power and yet they are power over against him which may destroy him and his neighbor. Such is the state of human nature that society has become the scene of the conflict of these powers, cajoled into tentative harmonies by necessity but breaking apart again into new conflicts, subjecting themselves to some more general and rational principle of the common interest, and then universalizing their own power by the use of reason, or by appeal to a moral principle of their own making. The task of the Christian is to help all politically aware men to expose the real powers at work behind these moral and rational facades in all their complexity and often sordidness so as to clarify the positive intention of God for the vitalities behind them.

Second, this means throwing oneself into the power conflict on the side of those forces in society which are working to lift up the disadvantaged, the poor and the excluded. This is the process which the Old Testament called "vindication" or "justification." This is a different matter from rejoicing in and manipulating the operation of countervailing power, though the development of such power in the political and economic process may be a part of it. It is also different from revolutionary action, though such action may be the channel it uses. It involves a witness to the legitimation of the power of the poor — black power, urban ghetto power, or the power of a revolutionary Third World — as an expression of God's covenant also with these people, and an exploration with them of the calling and the promise which grow out of it.

This cannot be done *for* the poor and the powerless by representatives of established, powerful and possessing classes, nations or races. It can only be done *with* them, and at times only by allowing them to accomplish it for themselves against us who belong to this establishment. Over a generation ago Reinhold Niebuhr observed that "men are no more able to eliminate self-interest from their nobler pursuits than they are able to express it fully without hiding it behind and compounding it with honest efforts at or dishonest pretensions of universality."[18] The rationality and the morality of the secure and the established can never be sufficiently aware of the

[18] *Moral Man and Immoral Society* (New York, 1932), p. 45.

justified claims of the poor and powerless unless they are forced to it by the effective opposition which these latter bring. Otherwise they will always tend to belittle the problem, and to conceal from themselves the self-interest contained in their own moral and rational concepts. To discern both the judgment and promise of God in this opposition, and to come to terms with it, requires an act of repentance, of renunciation out of which cooperation on the basis of equality may grow. For some Christians this will mean joining the revolutionaries and working within their choice of strategy and tactics. For others it will mean continuing responsibility for the sensitive exercise of established power, aware of its ambiguity and yet hopeful that a proper engagement of the poor in its exercise may yet render it creative.

The result of this will be that Christians will find themselves on opposite sides of lines of conflict, some working with one ideology, some with another, each questioning the other's analysis and choice of action. But this is the calling of the Church, to take the conflicts of the world up into itself and there subject them to a third member of the encounter, just as it is the calling of a Christian to face the judgment of God on his own system of order and peace, expressed through those who are excluded from it.

Third, the Christian is a witness to the relativity of the human power conflict and to the relations which transcend and transform it, and hence to the inherent limitations of coercive power to accomplish even the finest of ends. This is an empirically verifiable fact that threatens secular powers so strongly that they often forget it, but it goes to the heart of what the demythologizing of power as well the secular legitimation of power mean. Let me take from many examples three:

a. No amount of United States power has been able, in Vietnam, to create a democratic, peaceful, free society capable of responsible development. This is not because the counter power was too great. By any conventional measurement the American superiority in arms and money is overwhelming. It is not because tactical mistakes have been made, although they have, or because American personnel are not devoted to their task. It is rather because power itself reaches its limit in the effort to penetrate the heart of an alien culture and implant there a new idea which the people will adopt as their own self-image and their own future. If the Communists have been more successful than we, it is not because their coercive methods are more efficient or their terror more effective, but because they are more truly indigenous — the resisters rather than the organizers, dependent on the people for concealment and support, while offering them a hope which some at least could adopt as their own.

b. The struggle over urban planning in the United States has led to continual clashes between benevolent planners who wish the poor and the black community well — universities, federal, state and municipal agencies and the like — and the members of that community themselves. The planners have all the power this society offers — high-level expertise such as no group of poor people could bring forth, funds to carry projects through, and technology to build a transformed city. They can realize their plans regardless of the poor who are affected. But their very position of unmitigated power makes them helpless to win the trust and cooperation of those people.

49

It makes the price of freedom resistance to and destruction of the benevolent plan.

c. A revolution is in theory the uprising of masses of people, the assertion by the powerless of their power. Yet no sharper or more tragic conflict has arisen within the revolutionary movement of modern times than that between the strategy and tactics by which the leadership seek to conquer power on the one hand, and the desires and hopes of the masses on the other. Indeed it seems at times that only an incredible combination of brutality and incompetence in the opposition — a Czarist nobility, a Kuomintang, or a Battista — can hold them together. "The duty of every revolutionary is to make a revolution" was Che Guevara's slogan. Its meaning, expressed in his diaries and in Régis Debray's *Révolution dans la Révolution,* is clear. First comes the unit of power: the guerrilla group. Its tactics, its warfare, and the human relations developed in the struggle, are the basis for a strategic picture of the larger revolution and finally for an ideology. Only in the discipline of the power struggle itself does liberated man become aware of his own true destiny.

But it does not work that way. The result may be increasing failure of the masses to trust revolutionary power. "The peasant base is still not being formed," wrote Guevara with unconscious irony in his Bolivian diary, "although it seems that with planned terror we can neutralize most of them; support will come later." Or the result may be the success of a disciplined corps of ideologists who build their own ideal regardless of the masses, yet in their name — a success whose logic and conclusion were embodied in Stalin.

In all of these situations the wise action, even for the self-interest of the powerful themselves, would be to limit power by its creative renunciation, to cultivate, instead of overriding, effective opposition and to form policy by the participation of those affected. There is more hope for a Viet Cong dominated South Vietnam than for the present power combination; there is more future for a city which the people themselves slowly build up than for the most brilliant plan; there is more revolutionary wisdom in a people caught by a vision of their future than in the tightest guerrilla army. These insights are not beyond the capacity of secular human logic. Indeed, each power structure in our times pretends to build them into its own system: the Americans in Vietnam with their carefully controlled South Vietnamese government and elections, the city planners with their hand-picked consultants out of the community whose fate they are deciding, and the guerrilla movement with its liberation front. But the point at which insight breaks down and propaganda becomes furious in its effort to obscure reality is where the basic control of the power-holders is threatened, and with it the image of the world they hope to build or the structure they hope to maintain. The psychology of the builders of the Tower of Babel: "Come let us build ourselves a city and a tower with its top in the heavens, and let us make a name for ourselves lest we be scattered abroad upon the face of the earth" (Genesis 11:4) is still disastrously contemporary. That there is hope in being scattered abroad, that it is the suffering servant, struck down for the wrongs his power inflicted and given a new calling by God's forgiveness in his weakness, who will "not fail nor be discouraged till he has established justice in the earth and the coastlands wait for his law"

(Isaiah 42:4) — this is a truth which cannot be proved. Its promise can only be witnessed by those who have the faith to live it.

*   *   *

3. This brings us to the *final* proposition. The promise of God for this world, including its political structures, expresses itself through the discontinuity of human powers and securities, and institutions. In other words, the pattern of history is the pattern of the death and resurrection of its lord and redeemer. This seems to place the Christian message closer to the revolutionary than to the liberal planner or to the conserver of tradition. Richard Shaull builds his theology on this basic fact, and thus provides the American New Left with a more articulate theory than any other thinker. But this identification should not be made too simply. We have already seen that both liberal and revolutionary are aware of the death which threatens their hopes in the structures of violence which infect their own power. The nuclear balance of terror is only an instance of the situation. In every social conflict — the three mentioned above might also be cited — lies the ultimate measure that will destroy the future for both combatants. What then is the future beyond the end of the structures of meaning and the instruments of power with which both liberal and revolutionary now plan the future? In short, what can one count on to rise from the dead? The question is asked on all sides, even if the answer can only be risked in faith.

At this point politics itself depends on the witness of the Church. If there is hope in the renunciation of power, if something like a transforming reconciliation which changes both us and the enemy is a possible end to human conflict, if it is the reality which governs the future, then it is up to the Church to live this reality and in living it "to commend to the nations as practical politics the search for cooperation and peace." Our ethics will depend on the reality in which we believe.

CRITERIA FOR A JUST REVOLUTION

Ernest W. Lefever

Professor West has provided a perceptive and sympathetic profile of a contemporary revolutionary, one which fits a rather wide spectrum of articulate dissenters of the established order. His essay would be more satisfying if one could tell where the assorted revolutionaries he cites leave off and Mr. West begins. I have the impression that he is a selective and not a categorical revolutionary, though he seems broadly sympathetic toward revolutionary activity in the Third World and even in the United States.

It is not wholly clear where Mr. West stands on revolutionary activity within Red China, the Soviet Union, Cuba, and other Communist states.

If I understand his views, I find myself in substantial dissent in three areas: (1) the implied assumption that revolutionaries are more committed to justice and freedom than non-revolutionaries, (2) the character of American society and political institutions, and (3) the criteria for a justifiable revolution involving violence.

*   *   *

1. Change may be good or bad, depending upon its impact on the consequential issues of human freedom and justice

in a given historical situation. It is true that there is some injustice and unfreedom in every community and that every society would profit by constructive change. It is equally true that revolutionary change has often increased human suffering. If there is no moral presumption in favor of change, there is certainly none in favor of violent revolutionary change.

Mr. West's paper seems to assume that most revolutionaries are more committed to human rights than most non-revolutionaries, that the revolutionary is on the side of the "oppressed," and that somehow established political authority is the sole or principal "oppressor." Human beings being morally ambiguous, there are cynical, power-seeking revolutionaries, and humane, self-effacing establishmentarians. Lincoln was not a revolutionary and Stalin was. Our judgments must rest on moral and political standards which can distinguish between "good" and "bad" revolutionaries and non-revolutionaries.

The humane revolutionary and the humane non-revolutionary may differ profoundly on their reading of history and their understanding of how the cause of freedom and justice can be advanced. The argument between them should be joined on this level, and not be clouded by claims of self-righteousness by either side. Slogans and tactical differences should not be confused with moral commitment.

2. The United States today represents a profound achievement in man's long and tortured quest for a free and just political community. By virtually every test, American society is more open and mobile than that of any other state past or present. And because of the remarkable advances of the past three decades, there is no significant national legal or

governmental barrier to equality of opportunity for both the competitive and non-competitive minority groups in American society. Prejudice there is, but the law and the moral force of many non-government institutions are on the side of justice.

America has perhaps the most sensitive and responsive political system ever created. The will of a decisive majority can be forged quickly into effective law and policy. When the public mandate is not as clear, we have ample institutions, processes, and habits to move slowly in response to changes of the general will. Minority views are quickly registered by the political system. A prime example is the speedy rise of a relatively unknown man, Governor George Wallace. Within a very short time his party was listed on the ballot of the fifty states and he received a substantial vote in the 1968 presidential election. This development is a sign of health in the system. There is nothing in law or the system to prevent Senator Eugene McCarthy from taking over the Democratic Party or from leading a third, or a fourth, party. To be successful, all he needs is adequate support.

There are many Americans who insist that the U.S. Government spends too much on space exploration and national defense and too little on the cities. If these citizens want a shift in our "national priorities," they can bring it about by persuading a majority of their fellow citizens to join them. Free speech, a free press, the right to organize, and a very responsive political system can quickly and effectively translate any significant majority mandate into policy, domestic or foreign.

We must distinguish between the political system and current national policy. We should not fault the system for reflecting the public will. We should fault the system if it capitulated to minority pressures, however well intentioned they may be. If there is a confusion between policy (which may be good or bad) and the political system (which I hold to be basically just), there is also a confusion between policy and law, both of which are and should be responsive to the general will.

The Selective Service law, which is far from perfect, was not seriously questioned until there was an upsurge of protest against U.S. military involvement in South Vietnam. When Mr. West refers to a U.S. "law which compels men against their conscience" to "kill in Vietnam" he is badly informed. There is no such law. The Selective Service Act provides for conscientious participation or objection and gives each draftee at least four choices — regular military service, non-combat service, alternative civilian service, or prison. Three of these are clear options for a conscientious objector to combat service. Furthermore, this law will be changed when a clear majority of voting Americans want it changed.

Mr. West seems to confuse society with government. In this he is hardly alone. America is a highly pluralistic society with a multiplicity of institutions, a key one of which is, of course, the U.S. Government. Most of the ills of society — poverty, alcoholism, slaughter on the highways, race riots, student upheaval, automation, or cynicism — are not *caused* by the Government and cannot be cured by the Government. These and other ills have many roots, and the means available to the Government for dealing with them are severely limited. The political system does and should take appropriate steps to mitigate social problems, but government is not and should

57

not be regarded as a cure-all, except in a totalitarian state where the government claims to be omniscient and omnipotent.

In every society, however democratic, there is a lower twenty per cent in economic, educational, and cultural achievement — as well as an upper twenty per cent. As far as possible man-made barriers to equal opportunity should be eliminated. But many of the differences in station and achievement are inherent in the individual and his family situation. These conditions are not imposed by the system or the establishment. The dull cannot compete as well as the bright. The lazy cannot achieve as well as the industrious. In this country, the estabishment has gone to great lengths to make up for hereditary and environmental deficiencies by extensive welfare and educational programs for the physically, mentally, and socially handicapped. More can be done.

Mr. West seems to confuse contemporary America with Hitler's Germany, Stalin's Russia, Mao's China, Castro's Cuba, or present-day Russia. In terms of fair and equitable rules for living, competing, and resolving conflicting interests, the United States is far more advanced. It is now easier for a Negro to get into Harvard than it is for a white person of equal competence. Reverse discrimination is also widely practiced in government and business. This turn of events, while psychologically understandable in terms of overcompensating for past sins, should be carefully examined to see if it really contributes to justice either in the long or short run.

3. Abraham Lincoln said the people have a right to rise up in violence to overthrow a tyrannical or utterly corrupt regime if all the channels for peaceful redress of grievances have been closed and there is little prospect of opening them.

If this paraphrase embraces the essence of his position on political change, I find it wholly convincing. Mao Tse-tung has said that every people have a duty to make their own revolution, but he begs the question of who "the people" are. Do "the people" in Sinkiang have this duty today? Mao also advocated exporting violent revolution to assist in "wars of national liberation."

I too believe that people have a right to make their own revolutions if there is no peaceful way of overthrowing tyranny. By "people" I refer primarily to the population living under one political authority, i.e., a state. I oppose the "export" of revolutions just as I oppose wars of conquest and aggression. The people of a political community should throw out their own tyrants. It would have been much better for Germany and the world if the Germans had overthrown Hitler in 1936.

There are relatively just wars, relatively just revolutions, and relatively just status quos. In every case, the morally concerned observer must ask the question: "Will the prospect for freedom and justice be helped or hurt by the continuation of the status quo, by peaceful reform, or by the introduction of revolutionary violence?" Continuous adaption and change are needed in America in the interests of a more perfect union, but there is no need for revolution. All worthy objectives (insofar as the Government can contribute toward them) can be achieved peacefully, legally, and even quickly if there is a sufficient popular support for them.

One of the most precious achievements of American democracy is the rule of law — every citizen is under the same law and there are procedures for dealing with every grievance.

There is no place in America for any self-anointed elite that regards itself above the law because of the alleged righteousness of its cause. Capitulation to this pretension is the end of freedom.

Our system provides for majority rule which respects and guarantees the fundamental rights of all citizens, including those who break or disagree with current laws or who dissent from certain policies. This respect for the rights of the criminal and dissenter is rooted in the decency of Western man and enshrined in the U.S. Constitution. It finds expression in a thousand laws and supporting procedures. If the basic rights of the lowliest citizen are violated, he has multiple means of redress, though circumstances (not imposed by the system, but occurring in spite of it) may make it difficult for a poor man in a rural area to get a speedy determination of his case, unless "concerned" citizens take a special interest in him. And nothing in the system prevents effective expression of such human concern.

Neither the hard revolutionaries (Communists) nor the soft revolutionaries (utopians who naively insist on quick and drastic change without violence) understand the obligations and limits of political authority. If Washington is severely limited in what it can do within the arena of its sovereign jurisdiction, it is far more limited in the larger world. Our Government is criticized for not bringing democracy to South Vietnam. This lofty objective is beyond the political and moral competence of the U.S. Government or any other external agency. The invited United States presence in South Vietnam is not there for this purpose and, more important, the kind of government the South Vietnamese develop is their own business, not ours.

The United States is in South Vietnam not to reform the government, but to help provide a degree of security so the people of that tragic country can determine their own destiny without outside interference — in this case, primarily from Hanoi, massively supported by arms from Red China and Russia. These three governments — one directly and two indirectly — are engaging in aggression across an international frontier for the explicit purpose of overthrowing an existing government. Aggression against any state (whether it be South Vietnam, South Korea, Czechoslovakia, or East Germany) by another state is a flagrant violation of the most fundamental international law. This would be true even if the aggressor were a democratic state and the victim a Communist or fascist state.

Since the end of World War II the United States has pursued a general live-and-help-live policy toward small states endangered by aggression or external subversion and which have requested our assistance. Washington has emphasized peaceful change as the surest way toward greater justice and freedom. We have pursued policies designed to deter violence within and between states, believing that peace is more conducive to constructive social and political development than armed conflict.

Historically, political development has been slow and not always in a humane direction. The pace and character of political and social change are largely determined by indigenous factors. Even in the states receiving significant assistance from the United States, we have only a marginal influence. If we had the power, we should not attempt to make the world or even small patches of it over in our own image.

In sharp contrast to U.S. policy toward the Third World, the messianic and apocalyptic revolutionaries seek to destroy the present order, including many elements of justice within it, so they can build a new order. For them change has been too slow. They know the answer. They are arrogant. They cannot tolerate diversity. To be sure, the pragmatic revolt has had some impact upon overt Russian and Chinese tactics in the Third World, but the leaders of neither of these Communists giants have foresworn their absolute claim to be the wave of the future — a religious pretension without parallel in modern political history. According to these fanatics all peoples must be saved whether they want to be or not.

Our claim is more modest and our goals more limited. We simply claim that we, the American people, have a right to determine our political destiny. Our larger goal is a pattern of inter-state relations, a world order if you will, that respects this limited claim of self-determination for ourselves and for the peoples of all other states, large and small.

THE CHRISTIAN REVOLUTION AND ITS VIOLENCE

Monika Hellwig

As an educator, a theologian, and — it is to be hoped — some sort of a Christian, I find Charles C. West's paper to be pertinent, provocative and only the beginning of the discussion. One can only agree with him as to the task for Christian ethics in relation to violence and revolution in our times, and admire the way he sets out his arguments. My intent here is not to quibble over minor points, but to draw an axis through what seems to me the most forceful line of thought in a very complex presentation so as to contribute something further to the discussion.

Violence is indeed a highly ambiguous term with an elusive and variable meaning content. Explicitly or implicitly it is always defined within a frame of reference which is a particular understanding of the order of the world and of human history. Life consists of force and the application of force. When we use violence as a derogatory term, it designates the force that operates outside the accepted patterns of normalcy. As West points out, therefore, the preliminary task of a Christian ethic of revolution today is to attempt authentic dialogue between the establishment to which the ethicist usually belongs, and the revolutionary who confronts that establishment. The task involves critical analysis of the establishment ideology, coupled with sympathetic effort to penetrate the experience and ideology of those who reject the establishment because, materially or spiritually, they have no stake in it.

Attempting the first aspect of the task he has defined, West characterizes the American ethos as essentially conservative because it has consecrated its economic and political provisions for individual freedom and initiative, reducing God from transcendent judge to guarantor of the immanent process in which salvation is already assured. This insight seems to me powerful both as an interpretation of U.S. foreign policy and as an interpretation of our ability to tolerate with a clear conscience and in the name of freedom the most extreme and explosive inequities at home.

The presentation suggests, however, that this particular idolatry is already judged and ready for demythologization because the system is no longer viable. The turbulence of our cities and campuses and the increasingly questionable methods of our intervention in Vietnam are cited as but two examples among many. These examples indicate that what we define as normal in our theory is no longer something that we experience normally in practice. Violence, as we have defined it, is becoming the ordinary and routine experience of our society. The immanent process of empirical individualism towards ever-increasing personal freedom and fullfillment, demonstrably does not work. If I have correctly understood West, he is not suggesting that the American ethos and the structure that expresses it must be or will be totally rejected, but he does imply that the structure must be desacralized and relegated to its properly instrumental function before the establishment can be ready to dialogue or negotiate.

West pinpoints the revolutionary position as "that state of consciousness which defines the existing structure of law and order . . . as violence, and is devoted to its overthrow." The revolutionary is the negation of the system, not only passively in that he is its victim rather than its beneficiary, but also actively in that he puts himself in dynamic relation to the system in order to liberate men from its structures. And this he does in the name of a sometimes unnamed, or at least unspecified, hope. In the vocabulary of the revolutionary, whatever delays the liberation is defined as violence, whether or not it has been institutionalized by society. The propriety of the application of force is to be judged by its relation to the hoped-for future and not by its relation to the establishment of the present.

Precisely because so many Christian intellectuals are now inclined to passionate and unreflecting alignment with the revolutionary stance as West has here defined it, it seems to me of great importance that he goes on to give an excellent critique of the idolatry of the revolution. He asks the simple question as to what exactly is considered the hour of liberation. Clearly it has not come, and could not possibly come, at the moment of seizure of the machinery of power by the revolutionary force. At that point the task of the revolutionary to restore the disinherited really only begins, and is in fact a socially and economically complex task. But if alienation is a continuing fact, only slowly and relatively eliminated by a movement of dialogue and discovery of the common human base, the question arises whether and why the dialogic relationship cannot begin now — whether and why a takeover of the same sort and magnitude of power by a different group will in fact guarantee that the relationship between powerful and powerless will be transformed from one of deadly combat to one of easy and natural collaboration. Because the experience of the Communist countries has been so disillusioning, the revolutionary stance today is frequently anarchistic, aiming at the destruction of all centralized power. This raises the question that goes right back to the starting point of any revolutionary theory — whether a piecemeal program of protest and opposition within the structures of the establishment would not be the more effective way of dismantling the monolithic machinery of privilege and power, and forcing the structures to adapt to the demands of life.

From this starting point, West asks how we can discover the reality on which a viable public ethic may be based. He finds it not in an accomplished fact but in the covenantal relationship of man to the ultimate, the one God, who offers the community of all mankind as the fulfillment and freedom of each. It is a promise to be realized by the projection of tentative forms which it might take and the social task of organizing towards the projected realization. West sees political action and power as one of the forces necessarily involved in this task, not as an inevitable opposition to the Kingdom of God. He also expects of a government that it explicate and specify its ideology, that is, its understanding of the total public welfare and of the forms it projects for its realization. And he expects leaders in public opinion to maintain an open debate about that ideology which will flush out hidden interests and power groups behind policy decisions, and will question the horizons of the ideology itself.

West expects the Christian to enter directly into the power

struggle by throwing his weight "on the side of those forces in society which are working to lift up the disadvantaged, the poor and the excluded." But this clearly has to be done in ways that invite the renunciation of power, rather than backlash. It has to be done in ways which offer some possibility of success. In this, men of good will and wisdom, whether or not they hold the Christian worldview, will yet find themselves in disagreement in terms of their practical judgments and policies.

One must conclude from this presentation that the Christian cannot be the revolutionary of the pure type, because he cannot make the easy identification of the existing power structure with evil — evil is all that is not yet realized within himself and his own party as well as all that is lacking in the establishment for the full community of mankind. It seems to me that we Christians of the West are somewhat lacking in honesty if we do not admit that this would apply also to the Christian's attitude to a Communist state; the forces of evil may not be seen as concentrated simply in the Communist power structure, because this falsifies the nature and dimensions of the task. The Christian is committed to revolution quite concretely in the structures of this world, but it is a revolution in the finality and mode of all power.

In the same way, one must conclude that the other extreme of the spectrum is also closed to Christian loyalties. We cannot preach or practice simple obedience to the status quo, because it is no more than a partial achievement of a tentative projection of justice and of community. The Christian attitude is not that of the uncritical law-abiding citizen, not only because we can readily point to specific injustices in our present

67

society, but also because no governmental structure ever represents the end of the quest for justice or for the conditions of peace and community.

*   *   *

Speaking from Judeo-Christian postulates, it would seem that the *first* requirement of the Christian revolutionary is that he believe in the good faith of the other to the outer limits of possibility. Simple observation shows that most of us are busy most of the time trying to organize one another into such patterns as seem sensible to ourselves, without taking time out to ask whether they seem sensible to those we are trying to organize, and if not why not. Among religiously motivated liberals in our country today there is a good deal of intransigence and mistrust of one another as well as of the conservative opposition, with a resultant failure to achieve anything whatsoever. We had a shattering demonstration of it in the 1968 campaigning for the presidential primaries and the presidential elections. The mutual distrust and check-mating only served to consolidate a conservative force in the country and to exacerbate militant revolutionary feelings. Because this not only happened but could be clearly predicted beforehand, it can be judged an immoral use of power by the liberals. It is unethical in the fundamental understanding of the Judeo-Christian tradition because it is radically pessimistic and because it sees the evil as being always outside oneself and one's own group. It in no way tends towards community, and its refusal to do so is, by any standards of common sense, gratuitous.

A *second* requirement of the ethically revolutionary stance, as understood in the Judeo-Christian framework of the cove-

68

nantal relationship to the ultimate, is to allow not only one's particular policies but one's horizons to be challenged. There is no room within a covenantal understanding of history for an ideology in the hard sense, that is, for a predetermined ultimate form for human society. Neither communism nor capitalism, neither hereditary power nor Anglo-Saxon democracy, neither unions nor cooperatives, neither national sovereignty nor the United Nations can be canonized as the final answer.

But to let one's policies and horizons be challenged, while trusting the good faith of the other, implies a *third* principle, that of compromise. Not to be willing to search out the "doable" by compromise, is inevitably to set oneself up as the ultimate judge and once again to divide the world of men among the powers that work destruction.

One operates, of course, in a world where there is much violence, in the sense of what divides. To play the role of the prophet is no easy matter. There must be those who unmask the disguised violence that excludes some men from humanity. It is difficult to accomplish this task without aligning oneself with counter-violence that excludes the excluders. To counsel the Christian to steer clear of all situations where he must align himself with hate, would be to counsel him away from the task of championing the despised and underprivileged, for these latter usually hate their oppressors and accept as friends and helpers only those who share their hate. Men of the caliber of Mohandas Gandhi and Martin Luther King are not only rare but are seldom accepted as leaders by the disinherited. Yet the authentic spirit of the prophet is to seek a conversion of hearts and enlarging of vision in the oppressor, which will not result from a hardening of the lines of opposition. External violence, that is, violence directed against the other, will inevitably continue in the struggle, but within the ethical framework here supposed it can never be self-righteous. It has to be bitterly repentant even in the act itself, knowing that the measure of external violence is the measure in which the protest cannot possibly succeed in furthering true human community and therefore becomes self-defeating.

It should be quite clear that this applies not only to the violence one perpetrates oneself, but to the violence one evokes whether from one's own party or from the opposition. It would be facile to suppose that a mocking attitude, an insolent mode of "non-violent protest," is innocent of the uncontrolled physical violence it usually provokes from the establishment. To keep one's cool while evoking a display of anger from the other is the favorite and most damaging kind of aggression in use in our society. It is the most effective way of driving the opposition beyond the line of no return. This does not mean it is never strategically inevitable to adopt this stance. It does mean that it can only be taken with the deepest regret because the operation is then self-defeating.

True revolution by any standards is extremely difficult to accomplish. None could be a more powerful witness of this to our times than Nicolai Berdyaev, speaking out of his own experience of the Russian Revolution.[1] External force, force applied against the other, can never accomplish the revolution. The struggle is in the truest sense against the principalities and powers and not against flesh and blood, because there can be no revolution in the relations between men other

[1] Especially in *Dream and Reality* and *Slavery and Freedom*.

than a revolution within men. Our relationships, after all, are not external to ourselves; they constitute us.

In the Judeo-Christian understanding of what mankind's existence ultimately means, the essential violence of the essential revolution is that internal violence whose old-fashioned name is repentance or conversion of heart. It does, perhaps, need a new name because we are in a position to understand it better in the light of our explorations into inner space. We can see clearly now that it is not so much a question of turning towards a better fulfillment of the known demands, but of being open to a breaking of the horizon which contains those demands, and thus a reshaping of one's world. This is surely *metanoia*. The Jesuit theologian, Bernard Lonergan, has coined for it the new name of "major authenticity," the minor authenticity being the commensurate response within the existing horizon.[2]

In the light of the above observations, the ethical question may be addressed not so much to the policy that is adopted — for there may be many possible programs to rebalance inequities, any one of which would work if it received enough support — as to the mode in which it is proposed and implemented, and the quality of human relations which it fosters in its historical context. In this there is not much room for choice. Community is made by sharing, not by excluding, not even by excluding the excluders. It is more frequently achieved by listening, reflecting, voicing anxieties aloud, than by accusing. The same political platform can often be promoted in either mode.

[2] See "Existenz and Aggiornamento," in *Collection* (New York, 1967).

It may be objected that these reflections are unrealistic and have little to do with politics. But as West pointed out in his paper, we are already living at a rather highly developed stage of human awareness in which the "powers" are progressively being unmasked. In our own lifetime the idol of nationalism has begun to crumble even from the aspect of enlightened self-interest. The power of armed force is being revealed as severely limited by psychic reality. We have tried to make a science and an art out of human relations, which we have recognized as a vital factor in politics, economics, diplomacy and warfare. We are ready to admit that the values by which we ourselves really live, individually and in groups, are the values we are most likely to communicate to others. In spite of specific testimonies to the contrary, it is beginning to look as though the land may, after all, go to the meek.